PAULIST BIBLE STUDY PROGRAM

# Isaiah: The Message, The Vision

## WORKBOOK

Workbook by Chris Franke
Video Scripts by Patrick Griffin, C.M.
Prayers by Michael H. Marchal

PAULIST PRESS

New York/Mahwah

## Acknowledgments

Cover photo, *Pilgrims approaching Jerusalem*, courtesy of Bridgeman/Art Resource, NY.

Excerpts from the English translation of *The Roman Missal* © 1973, International Committee on English in the Liturgy, Inc. (ICEL); excerpts from the English translation of *Rite of Penance* © 1974, ICEL; excerpts from the English translation of *Rite of Confirmation*, Second Edition © 1975, ICEL. All rights reserved.

Psalm texts are reprinted from *Psalms Anew: In Inclusive Language* compiled by Nancy Schreck, O.S.F. and Maureen Leach, O.S.F., copyright © 1986 by St. Mary's Press, Winona, MN. Used by permission.

Faith Sharing Principles are reprinted from RENEW, copyright © 1987 by the Roman Catholic Archdiocese of Newark, New Jersey. Used by permission.

ISBN: 0-8091-9414-7

Published by Paulist Press
997 Macarthur Boulevard
Mahwah, New Jersey 07430

Printed and bound in the United States of America

Dear Friends,

It is a pleasure to present to you our Paulist Bible Study Program. The Paulist Bible Study Program is designed to help adults understand the Bible in the light of contemporary biblical scholarship and to use the Bible as a source of prayer, reflection, and action. It relates the study of the Bible to the liturgy, to the Church, and to our daily lives. Those who long to know more about the Bible, based on the authentic Catholic tradition and the most responsible and best biblical scholarship, have a rich experience awaiting them.

Kevin A. Lynch, C.S.P.
Publisher

## INTRODUCTION

Welcome to the Paulist Bible Study Program and to this fourth unit on the Old Testament.

In this unit you will study the Book of Isaiah, perhaps the most influential of all the prophetic books of the Bible. This Workbook will serve as a reading guide to the Bible and to your companion text, *Isaiah of Jerusalem*, by William J. Doorly. Each week it will point out what passages of the Bible you should read and what parts of the companion text are focused on these passages.

### The Bible in the Life of the Church

The emergence of popular interest in the Bible among Catholics stems from the Second Vatican Council. Along with the new emphasis on the Scriptures during the Eucharist and other sacramental celebrations, the Council called upon all members of the Church to grow in their knowledge and love of the Bible:

> Just as the life of the Church grows through persistent participation in the Eucharistic mystery, so we may hope for a new surge of spiritual vitality from intensified veneration for God's Word (*Dogmatic Constitution on Divine Revelation*, 26).

The vision of the central place of the Scriptures which the Council set forth is becoming more and more a reality.

> The Church has always venerated the divine Scriptures just as she venerates the body of the Lord, since from the table of both the Word of God and of the body of Christ she

unceasingly receives and offers to the faithful the bread of life, especially in the sacred liturgy. She has always regarded the Scriptures together with sacred tradition as the supreme rule of faith, and will ever do so (*Dogmatic Constitution on Divine Revelation*, 21).

## Reading the Old Testament

As you begin your study of this portion of the Old Testament, it is helpful to keep in mind these words of the Council:

> In carefully planning and preparing the salvation of the whole human race, the God of supreme love, by a special dispensation, chose for Himself a people to whom He might entrust His promises....The plan of salvation, foretold by the sacred authors, recounted and explained by them, is found as the true Word of God in the books of the Old Testament: these books, therefore, written under divine inspiration, remain permanently valuable (cf. Rom 15:4; *Dogmatic Constitution on Divine Revelation*, 14).

Throughout this program we use the term Old Testament rather than Hebrew Scriptures. For Christians, this has been the traditional title through the centuries. It is important for us as Christians to recognize that we cannot use the term Old Testament in a way that is condescending to Judaism. Our faith is rooted in Judaism and the Old Testament remains "permanently valuable," not only as a foreshadowing of the New, but because in itself it contains the "true Word of God."

## Jesus' Own Bible Study Model

In 1986, Archbishop Roger Mahony of Los Angeles issued a pastoral letter entitled "The Bible in the Life of the Church." One part of the letter reflects on Jesus' own approach to teaching the Scriptures to his disciples as he walked with two of them on the road to Emmaus (Lk 24:13-35). Archbishop Mahony's reflections on this passage are a fitting introduction to our study of the Bible.

> The two disciples are on their way from Jerusalem to Emmaus when Jesus—his appearance hidden—joins them. He responds to their bewilderment by "interpreting for them every passage of Scripture which referred to him." This was the most clear example of Jesus sharing the Scriptures that we find in the gospels. For our own Bible study to be beneficial, then, we too must open our hearts and lives to allow Jesus to unlock the meaning of his message for us.

> But two additional elements in the Emmaus journey are also required to validate our own experience of the Scriptures. First, our Scripture study must lead toward, center around, and flow from the Eucharist—the Mass. It was only in "the breaking of the bread" that the full meaning of Jesus' explanations became clear to the two men journeying to Emmaus. As Catholics, we too must always focus our Bible studies in and through the Eucharist. And secondly, we must be guided in our Scripture studies through "Simon Peter—the Church." Recall that the two men returned in haste to Jerusalem where they were greeted with: "The Lord has been raised! It is true! He has appeared to Simon." This validation by Peter—by the Church—is essential to our authentic understanding of the Word of God.

## The Importance of Commitment

What are your goals for your participation in this program? Any goal worth achieving requires commitment. During this program you are invited to make a commitment to grow in your understanding and appreciation of the Bible. All commitments require the most precious of commodities: time. In this case, you are committing yourself to be present at the eight sessions and to participate in the learning process.

What follows is a description of the various steps you should take to prepare for and to follow up on a meeting. Only you can determine how much time you have to spend on these steps. Not everything needs to be done now. Hopefully, the Paulist Bible Study Program will provide you with the resources to continue your own study well after a particular unit ends.

## Preparing for the Meeting

Each week you will be meeting with others to reflect on the Scriptures and the parts of the companion text. Before you engage in the activities in this book, follow the steps outlined for each session in the section called Preparation.

1. Prayerfully read the appointed Bible passages.

2. Read the assigned portion of the companion text. You may want to read a little bit each day to coordinate with your prayerful reading of the Bible. Many find it helpful to mark the text for key parts or to jot down questions that may arise during a reading.

3. Read the Focus and Review of Contents before the meeting. If you have time, try to work on responses to the review questions/activities. Your companion text also has review questions after each chapter which will be helpful.

## During the Meeting

Each session is designed to last two hours. You may find that the suggested times for each element vary for your group. Encourage the sharing and interaction within your group rather than feeling bound by time. Here are the steps for each session and some suggestions on how to make use of them.

*Opening Prayer* (5 minutes)
Place yourself and your group in God's presence, asking for the guidance of the Holy Spirit during the upcoming session.

*Review of Contents* (25 minutes)
This section gives you the opportunity to express what you have learned and to learn from the insights of others. If you have questions other than those raised in the review, bring them up at this time. While your Program Leader cannot be expected to have all the answers, he or she may be able to help you find the answers to your questions.

*Video* (20 minutes)

The video is designed to enrich your learning by providing the visual dimension of what you are studying. Before viewing the program, look at the highlight questions. Jot down the answers as you watch the program. Afterward, there is a brief time for you to raise questions or make a comment.

*Learning Activity* (25 minutes)

During this segment, you will work with others in an activity to further integrate the meaning of the Scripture you have read and to apply it to your life.

*Faith Sharing* (25 minutes)

The following suggestions, borrowed from RENEW, are helpful guidelines for faith sharing:

• The entire faith-sharing process is seen as prayer, i.e., listening to the Word of God as broken by others' experience.
• Constant attention to respect, honesty, and openness for each person will assist the group's growth.
• Each person shares on the level where he or she feels comfortable.
• Silence is a vital part of the total process of faith sharing. Participants are given time to reflect before any sharing begins, and a period of comfortable silence might occur between individual sharings.
• Persons are encouraged to wait to share a second time until others who wish to do so have contributed.
• The entire group is responsible for participating and faith sharing.
• Confidentiality is essential, allowing each person to share honestly.
• Reaching beyond the group in action and response is essential for the growth of individuals, the group, and the Church.

*Closing Prayer* (10 minutes)

Having shared our faith together, we conclude with prayer. Join in the spirit of the prayer service by singing, praying, and listening to the Word of God.


## After the Meeting

*Journaling*

For each session, at least one journal idea is suggested. You may wish to keep a journal either to do these activities, or simply to write your own reflections.

*Additional Resources*

Each week a number of sources are referred to for further reading and study. Your parish may have purchased these books for a parish resource library or you may obtain them from Paulist Press. Your Program Leader has further information. You may wish to consult these sources for continued study after the unit ends.

# 1. The Divisions of the Book of Isaiah

## Preparation

- Read Doorly, Introduction, "The Divisions of the Book of Isaiah"; Chapter 1, "The Role of the City of Jerusalem in the Emergence and Growth of First Isaiah"; and Chapter 2, "The Prologue to the Book of Isaiah."
- Read Isaiah 7:1–9, 37:1–7, 38:1–8; and Isaiah 1.
- Reflect on the FOCUS statement.

Ordinarily, you are expected to do the Preparation assignments before the group meeting on that session. It is important to the success of this program that you do so. In the case of the first session, however, it is possible that not every participant had the information or the resources available to do the reading beforehand. Accordingly, the structure of this particular session allows an individual who was unable to do the readings to participate fully in the meeting nonetheless.

---

### FOCUS

In this session we will be introduced to the Book of Isaiah, perhaps the most influential of all the prophetic books in the Bible. Even though this book is named after Isaiah of Jerusalem, it includes much more than the words of this eighth-century prophet. In fact, the three major divisions of the Book of Isaiah span a period of more than two centuries. We will find that within this one book of the Bible there are several strikingly different points of emphasis, distinct images of God, and a variety of ways of talking about the future.

The oracles of all of the eighth-century prophets—Amos, Hosea, Isaiah, and Micah—have undergone a process of extensive editing over the centuries. The period of editing lasted through the time of the exile into the sixth century. We will learn about how and why these texts were edited, and by whom.

## OPENING PRAYER

### Call to Prayer

*Leader:*
Isaiah proclaimed:
"O house of Jacob, come,
let us walk in the light of the LORD!" (Is 2:5)

(Leader lights the candle.)

Jesus is the light of the world!

*All:*
The light no darkness can ever extinguish!

### Responsorial Psalm (Ps 147; cf. 1 Cor 3:17)

*Leader:*
The Psalms speak for us in prayer. Our refrain will be:
The temple of God is holy, and we are that temple!

*All:*
The temple of God is holy, and we are that temple!

*Leader:*
Glorify Yahweh, O Jerusalem;
praise your God, O Zion.

For God has strengthened the bars of your gates
and has blessed your children within you.

*All:*
The temple of God is holy, and we are that temple!

*Leader:*
God has granted peace on your borders
and fills you with the best of wheat.
God sends forth a command to the earth;
swiftly runs the word!

*All:*
The temple of God is holy, and we are that temple!

*Leader:*
God scatters hail like crumbs;
before God's cold, the waters freeze.
God sends a word and melts them;
God lets the breeze blow and the waters flow.

*All:*
The temple of God is holy, and we are that temple!

*Leader:*
God's word has been proclaimed to Jacob,
laws and decrees to Israel.
God has not done this for any other nation;
God has not made such laws known to them.

*All:*
The temple of God is holy, and we are that temple!
Glory be to the Father,
and to the Son,
and to the Holy Spirit.
As it was in the beginning,
is now, and will be forever. Amen.

## Prayer

*Leader:*
Let us pray quietly that each of us might have a deeper sense of what a great gift God's Word is. (Pause for a whole minute of reflection.)

*All:*
Blessed are you,
We thank you, Lord our God,
Creator of the universe, Father of Jesus!
In him the age-old longing of your people
has been fulfilled.
A new age has dawned;
the long reign of sin has ended;
a broken world has been renewed.
Anoint us once again with your Spirit,
until we proclaim the good news of Jesus
to all humankind
and the whole earth is filled with his glory.
For he is Lord, now and forever. Amen.

# GETTING STARTED

1. Your group leader will introduce you to the first division of the Book of Isaiah. This division relates to a specific historical period, and a particular geographical location. Make note of the following:

The chapters of First Isaiah: _____.

The historical period associated with First Isaiah:
_____ B.C.

The location associated with First Isaiah:

_____.


2. The last part of the Book of Isaiah is related to other times and places. Make note of these divisions in the Book of Isaiah:

The chapters of Second Isaiah: _____.

The historical period associated with Second Isaiah:
_____ B.C.

The location associated with Second Isaiah:

_____.

The chapters of Third Isaiah: _____.

The historical period associated with Third Isaiah:
_____ B.C.

The location associated with Third Isaiah:

_____.


3. Your group leader will introduce you to the eighth-century prophets and will talk about how their words came to be written down and preserved through the centuries. There are four eighth-century prophets. Their names are as follows:

a. _____

b. _____

c. _____

d. _____


4. The books of these eighth-century prophets are similar to one another in that each shows evidence of having been edited (or redacted) in a later period. There are three major stages common to the composition of each of these books. Each stage addresses a different audience. Identify each stage, and the audience for each stage.

a. first stage:

   audience:

b. second stage:

   audience:

c. third stage:

   audience:

## VIDEO

An Overview of the Book of Isaiah

As you view the video, please make note of the following:

1. Why is the Book of Isaiah considered so influential?

_____

_____

2. What elements characterize prophetic writing?

_____

_____

3. How do the messages of the authors of Isaiah differ?

_____

_____

## BREAK
(10 minutes)

# LEARNING ACTIVITY

## Guidelines for Discussion

In this and in subsequent Learning Activities, it will be helpful to observe the following guidelines:

- Learning is a collaborative adventure, not a competition.
- Each person should be encouraged to take part in the discussion. No one person should be allowed to monopolize the group's time.
- The aim of group discussion is understanding what each group member is saying rather than jumping in to argue or defend your point of view.
- If you would like clarification, try restating what you think was said so that the other person can let you know whether you understood correctly.
- If your point of view differs from that of someone else, state what you believe and the reasons why. Remember that there are times when there is more than one correct way to answer a question.

1. Have a member of the group read aloud the following passages from Isaiah of Jerusalem. How is God portrayed in the passage? Who are the evildoers? What does the future hold for these people?

– Isaiah 1:2–4, 7–8

– Isaiah 3:13–14, 25–26

– Isaiah 10:1–4


– Isaiah 28:1–3



2. Have someone in the group read the following passages from Isaiah 40–66. Discuss how God is portrayed and what is in the future for these people.

– Isaiah 40:1–2


– Isaiah 43:1–3


– Isaiah 44:26


– Isaiah 66:10–13



3. Make two lists in which you compare the images of God in Isaiah of Jerusalem with the images in Isaiah 40–66. Discuss the ways in which these images are similar to and different from one another.

ISAIAH OF JERUSALEM                    ISAIAH 40–66

# FAITH SHARING

## Guidelines for Sharing

- Faith sharing is not a discussion. As the word makes clear, persons simply share with others their beliefs, experiences, feelings, and dreams. We receive the sharings of others with a loving and respectful attention— with gratitude that other human beings have gifted us with parts of their own inner life.
- One person's sharing may remind you about something in your own experience which you would like to share. However, you are asked to talk only about yourself, not to comment on what other persons have shared.
- This is not the time to analyze other persons' problems or give them advice.
- Matters shared in these activities should be treated as confidential and not discussed outside of your group.

During this session you learned that the Book of Isaiah contains the ideas and thoughts of a variety of people and reflects several different time periods. You saw that through the years the words of one prophet influenced the thinking of people who were not part of his original audience, and that the message of this prophet came to be reinterpreted by people in later years so that the words could speak to the changed situation of the audience.

Jot down some examples of different ideas of God you have had over the years. Has your way of thinking about God changed in response to crises or transitions in your life? How?

Share with the people in your group how your idea of God has changed (or remained stable) over the course of your lifetime, and how this experience relates to the different images of God which exist in the Book of Isaiah.

# CLOSING PRAYER

## Hearing the Word

*Leader:*
God's covenant with his people is not ultimately founded on a special place like Jerusalem or a special family like David's but on his never-failing love for his people. Let us listen to part of the conversation between Jesus and the Samaritan woman at the well and ask ourselves how Jesus is challenging our preconceptions in this passage.

## Reading

(All stand, facing the reader, in anticipation of the challenge Jesus poses.)

*Reader* (picking up the large Bible):
A reading from the gospel according to John (4:19–26).

## The Offering of Incense and Shared Prayer

## Concluding Prayer

*Leader:*
Let us join our hands and pray together the Our Father.

*All:*
Our Father, . . .
For the kingdom, etc.

*Leader:*
O house of Jacob, come;
let us walk in the light of the Lord
now and forever and ever.

*All:*
Amen.

# FOLLOW-UP

## A. Journaling

1. In your group, people talked about their images of God. Perhaps you found that some of you had radically different ways of thinking about God. Do you prefer a church or community in which all people hold the same image or idea of God, or one in which people disagree about how to talk and think about God? Consider what happens when people do not think about God in the same way; reflect upon what it would be like if everyone agreed upon an image of God.

2. Isaiah 40:10–11 describes God coming to comfort his people as both a mighty warrior bringing a reward to his suffering people, and as a gentle shepherd, feeding his flock and tenderly guiding them. Write about the times in your life when you have wanted God to come to your aid as a powerful warrior; then, write about when you have sought out God as a gentle shepherd. How do different situations in your life affect the way you pray to God?

## B. Additional Resources

1. Read Amos, Chapters 4:1–5, 5:10–12, 6:1–7 for an example of the evils of the day which the eighth-century prophets condemned. See the footnoted commentary in *The Catholic Study Bible*, pp. 1129-1132.

2. Read Margaret Nutting Ralph, *Plain Words About Biblical Images*, "Foreword," pp. 1–14, on how imagery is used in the Bible, and how our use of images changes as our faith develops.

3. Read John W. Miller, *Meet the Prophets: A Beginner's Guide to the Books of the Biblical Prophets*, Chapter 9, "Isaiah, Son of Amoz," pp. 90–104.

# 2. Assyrian Domination and the Early Oracles

## Preparation

- Read Doorly, Chapter 3, "The Domination of the Near East by Assyria," and Chapter 4, "Early Oracles."
- Read Isaiah 7 and 2 Kings 16; and Isaiah 2–5.
- Reflect on the FOCUS statement and REVIEW OF CONTENTS questions.

---

**FOCUS**

The words of Isaiah of Jerusalem cannot be understood outside of their historical context. Since Isaiah first spoke to people who were very much aware of the Assyrian Empire and its control over their lives, today's readers must learn about that world in order to better understand the message of Isaiah.

In this session we will learn about the Assyrian Empire and its control of the fertile crescent. We will see the variety of resources both within the Bible and apart from it which are available to interested readers who would like to know more about the world of Isaiah. We will also become familiar with the early oracles of Isaiah of Jerusalem in Chapters 2–5. While these oracles are for the most part proclamations of doom upon a sinful people, two of them do promise a hopeful future for a transformed community of believers.

---

# OPENING PRAYER

## Call to Prayer

*Leader:*
Isaiah proclaimed:
"For over all [of Mount Zion]
God's glory will be shelter and protection." (Is 4:6)

(Leader lights the candle.)

Jesus is the light of the world!

*All:*
The light no darkness can ever extinguish!

## Scripture (Jn 15:1–2)

*Leader:*
Let us listen as the Word of God speaks to us.

Jesus said to his disciples:
"I am the true vine, and my Father is the vine grower. He takes away every branch in me that does not bear fruit, and everyone that does he prunes so that it bears more fruit."

## Responsorial Psalm (Is 5:7; Ps 80)

*Leader:*
Our refrain will be: The vineyard of the Lord is the house of Israel!

*All:*
The vineyard of the Lord is the house of Israel!

*Leader:*
Hear me, O Shepherd of Israel!
You who guide Joseph like a flock.
Enthroned on the cherubs, shine out
on Ephraim, Benjamin, and Manasseh.

*All:*
The vineyard of the Lord is the house of Israel!

*Leader:*
Rouse your power and come to save us!
Restore us, Yahweh.
We will be secure when you smile upon us.

*All:*
The vineyard of the Lord is the house of Israel!

*Leader:*
From Egypt you uprooted a vine;
to plant it you scattered other nations.
You cleared a space so it could flourish,
and it took root and filled the land.

*All:*
The vineyard of the Lord is the house of Israel!

*Leader:*
Why have you leveled its fences?
Now all can pluck its fruit.
The wild boar can trample it,
and wild beasts devour it.

*All:*
The vineyard of the Lord is the house of Israel!

*Leader:*
O Yahweh, please return!
Look down from heaven and see this vine.
Nurture and guard what your hand has planted.

*All:*
The vineyard of the Lord is the house of Israel!

*Leader:*
Never again will we turn away from you;
we shall call on your holy name with a renewed spirit.
Restore us, Yahweh Sabaoth;
let your face smile on us—
then we will be safe.

*All:*
The vineyard of the Lord is the house of Israel!

**Prayer**

*Leader:*
God's Word can bear abundant fruit only if everything that keeps us from love is pruned away. Let us pray quietly that we might understand what God might need to prune in us personally. (Pause for a whole minute of reflection.)

*All:*
Blessed are you,
We thank you, Lord our God,
Creator of the universe, Father of Jesus!
In him the age-old longing of your people
has been fulfilled.
A new age has dawned;
the long reign of sin has ended;
a broken world has been renewed.
Anoint us once again with your Spirit,
until we proclaim the good news of Jesus
to all humankind
and the whole earth is filled with his glory.
For he is Lord, now and forever. Amen.

# REVIEW OF CONTENTS

1. Identify some of the characteristics of the Assyrian rulers during the days of Isaiah of Jerusalem.

2. Where does the Bible talk about the Assyrian presence in Palestine during the second half of the eighth century? What other sources help us to understand the important role which Assyria played during this time?

3. Summarize the contents of the early oracles of Isaiah of Jerusalem (Chaps. 2–5). Which of these oracles were hopeful in tone, and what was the content of that hope? Which of the oracles delivered bad news, and what was the nature of that news?

4. What social problems did Isaiah address in the woe oracles?

5. Isaiah's words in these early oracles are very similar to those of two other eighth-century prophets. Name those prophets and show the similarities with Isaiah.

## VIDEO

The Reasons Behind Assyrian Domination

As you view the video, please make note of the following:

1. How did Assyria triumph over its enemies?

_____

_____

2. What abuses did the prosperity of Judah bring about?

_____

_____

3. Did Isaiah view Assyria as a problem or as a solution? Why?

_____

_____

## BREAK
(10 minutes)

# LEARNING ACTIVITY

1a. Have someone in your group read aloud from 2 Kings 16:1–4. Answer the following questions after the reader finishes:

Which king is the main focus of these verses? Of which nation is he king? How does this king compare to his ancestor, David? What are some of the activities of this king which are mentioned in this passage?

b. Have another person in the group continue reading aloud the narrative in 2 Kings 16:5–9. Answer the following questions:

Who are the four kings introduced in this passage, and which country did each rule? Which of these kings, if any, is friendly toward Judah? Which is unfriendly? What action does the king of Judah take to extricate himself from the threat of attack? What is the outcome?

2a. Have someone from your group read Isaiah 7:1–2.

What additional details about the Syria-Israel coalition against Judah do these verses contain?

b. Have someone else in the group read Isaiah 7:3–7. Answer the following questions:

Whom does God tell Isaiah to go and meet? What is the message which Isaiah is supposed to deliver? What do

Syria and Israel plan to do once they have conquered Judah? Will this plan succeed?

3a. Have someone in the group read the first part of the woe oracles in Chapter 5 (vv. 8–17). Answer the following questions:

What specific actions does the prophet criticize? What will the punishment for these actions be? Is there any connection between the offense and the punishment?

b. Have another in your group read the second part of the woe oracles in Chapter 5 (vv. 18–25). Consider the series of questions above in reference to these oracles.

# FAITH SHARING

A perspective shared by Isaiah of Jerusalem, many other prophets, and Deuteronomic theology is summed up in the following words from Isaiah 3:10–12:

Happy the just, for it will be well with them,
   the fruit of their works they will eat.
Woe to the wicked man! All goes ill,
   with the work of his hands he will be repaid.

1. Can you think of examples from your own life or from the lives of others in which this principle held true? Share examples with the people in your group about when a good person has enjoyed the fruits of her or his works, or when evil deeds have resulted in just punishment.

2. Can you think of examples in which this principle did not hold true? Are there examples of good people being unjustly treated, or unjust people living rewarding lives? Share your examples and explore together the reactions to such situations.

3. Do you think that the viewpoint of Isaiah on reward and punishment is one which holds meaning for people of today? Why or why not?

# CLOSING PRAYER

## Hearing the Word

*Leader:*
As we listen to God's Word from the gospel of Luke, part
of the  passage might be very familiar and part rather
unsettling. Let us ask ourselves how Jesus is challenging us
and our society to reexamine our priorities in life.

## Reading

(All stand, facing the reader.)

*Reader* (picking up the large Bible):
A reading from the gospel according to Luke (6:17–26).

## Litany of Healing

*Leader:*
Let us pray to the Lord.

*All:*
Lord Jesus, touch us with your power, and heal us all!

## Concluding Prayer

*Leader:*
Lord our God, Father of Jesus,
your sons and daughters pray to you in humility and trust.
Look with love on us and on our world;
heal our wounds; save us and raise us up.
For we are members of Christ's body;
the sheep of your flock, children of your family.
Show us the way of holiness,
and bring us to true peace in your kingdom.
We make this prayer in the power of the Spirit
through Christ who is Lord forever and ever.

*All:*
Amen.

*Leader:*
Over all of Mount Zion,
God's glory will be shelter and protection
now and forever and ever.

*All:*
Amen.

## FOLLOW-UP

### A. Journaling

1. In the readings for this session, we saw that Isaiah was extremely critical of those in power in Israel and Judah who used their position to advance themselves at the expense of the poor. Using the woe oracles of Isaiah 5:8–25 as a guide, write your own set of oracles for a twentieth-century audience. As you write, think about who your audience is, what the offenses are, and what kinds of consequences a prophet would announce for these offenses.

2. Isaiah (and Micah) imagined a world in which peace triumphs because of the transforming power of human nature. Write about what it would mean today in your community, city, state, or country if "swords were turned into plowshares, spears into pruning hooks." Is there any "sword" or "spear" in your life that you can turn into a "plowshare"? Write about how you could help to turn things of destruction and violence into life-giving resources.

### B. Additional Resources

1. Read 2 Kings 17–20 to fill out the story of Assyrian involvement in Israel and Judah during the time of Isaiah's prophetic ministry.

2. Read John W. Miller, *Meet the Prophets: A Beginner's Guide to the Books of the Biblical Prophets*, Chapter 10, "His Message and Its Relevance," pp. 105–121.

# 3. The Memoirs of Isaiah

## Preparation

- Read Doorly, Chapter 5, "The Memoirs of Isaiah," and Chapter 6, "The Memoirs of Isaiah (Continued)."
- Read Isaiah 6–8:15.
- Reflect on the FOCUS statement and REVIEW OF CONTENTS questions.

---

**FOCUS**

In this session we will examine the account of Isaiah's vision in the temple and his relationship with King Ahaz of Judah, as recorded in Chapters 6–8 (also referred to as Isaiah's memoirs). There are several puzzling issues in these chapters. Among them is the question of whether or not Isaiah's vision in the temple was his call to be a prophet. Another question concerns the nature of King Ahaz's relationship with Assyria.

Among the many ways that Isaiah (and other prophets such as Hosea) communicated with his audience was by the use of symbolic names. We will read about several of these names, including the mysterious Immanuel, as well as the names of Isaiah's own children.

Finally, we will reflect on the way people reacted to the prophet Isaiah and the way we might react today if confronted by someone claiming to be speaking for God.

---

# OPENING PRAYER

## Call to Prayer

*Leader:*
Jesus proclaimed:
"I came into the world as light, so that everyone who
believes in me might not remain in darkness." (Jn 12:46)

(Leader lights the candle.)

Jesus is the light of the world!

*All:*
The light no darkness can ever extinguish!

## Scripture (Is 6:1b, 2a, 3)

*Leader:*
Let us listen to Isaiah and complete his words with a sung
refrain of "Holy, holy, holy."

"I saw the Lord seated on a high and lofty throne, with the
train of his garment filling the temple. Seraphim were sta-
tioned above; they cried one to the other:

*All:*
Holy, holy, holy...

## Psalm (Ps 147:7–11)

*Leader:*
Sing to God with thanksgiving;
sing praise with the harp to our God,
who covers the heavens with clouds,
who provides rain for the earth,
and who makes grass grow on the mountains,

who gives food to the cattle,
and to the young ravens when they call.

God does not delight in the strength of the steed,
nor is God pleased with the fleetness of humans.
God is pleased with those who have reverence,
with those who hope in faithful love.

*All:*
Glory be to the Father,
and to the Son,
and to the Holy Spirit.
As it was in the beginning,
is now, and will be forever. Amen.


## Prayer

*Leader:*
Let us pray quietly for a richer awareness of God's constant
presence with us. (Pause for a whole minute of reflection.)

*All:*
Blessed are you,
We thank you, Lord our God,
Creator of the universe, Father of Jesus!
In him the age-old longing of your people
has been fulfilled.
A new age has dawned;
the long reign of sin has ended;
a broken world has been renewed.
Anoint us once again with your Spirit,
until we proclaim the good news of Jesus
to all humankind
and the whole earth is filled with his glory.
For he is Lord, now and forever. Amen.

# REVIEW OF CONTENTS

1. Outline the various opinions of scholars on the meaning of Isaiah's vision in the temple (Is 6). Was it for the purpose of (a) calling Isaiah to the prophetic office or (b) changing the direction of Isaiah's ministry?

2. Write one or two phrases in which you identify each of the following:

– Samaria

– Jerusalem

– Damascus

– the Syro-Ephraimite coalition

– Ephraim

– Tiglath-pileser III

– Ahaz

– "this people"

– Immanuel

– the house of David

3. Did Ahaz ask Assyria for help against Pekah and Rezin? In answering this question, explain why there are disagreements among scholars as to a definitive answer.

## VIDEO

Isaiah and Ahaz

As you view the video, please make note of the following:

1. What dilemma did Israel and Damascus pose to Judah?

_____

_____

2. What did the first so-called Immanuel prophecy mean
for those in Isaiah's time? For those in the New Testament?

_____

_____

3. Identify the significance of two prophetic images Isaiah
uses in his words of caution to Ahaz.

_____

_____

**BREAK**
(10 minutes)

# LEARNING ACTIVITY

1. Based on your careful reading of the following passages, answer the accompanying questions:

a. Isaiah 6:1–5

– Where did the vision take place?

– How did Isaiah describe God?

– Describe the seraphim and their activities.

– What else happened during this vision?

– How did Isaiah first respond to this experience?

b. Isaiah 6:6–8

– How did the seraphim respond to Isaiah's cry of woe?

– What did God say after this happened to Isaiah?

– How did Isaiah respond to this experience?

c. Isaiah 6:9–13

– After Isaiah volunteered to be God's messenger, what did God tell him?

– How did Isaiah respond?

– What was God's answer?

– Compare Isaiah's initial response to the vision to his response after his encounter with the seraphim and with God.

2a. Ask members of your group who have different translations of the Bible to read Isaiah 7:14 aloud. Listen carefully and note in your Workbook the places where your translation differs from what you heard. What are the differences among the various translations?

b. Ask the members of the group to read the footnotes in their Bible which refer to this passage. What do you learn about this passage from these notes?

3. Elsewhere in Isaiah, and in Hosea, another eighth-century prophet, children are given symbolic names. Look at the following passages and identify those names and their meanings. You may have to consult the footnotes in your Bible to find the meanings of some names.

– Isaiah 7:3

– Isaiah 8:1–4

– Hosea 1:4

– Hosea 1:6

– Hosea 1:8

– Hosea 2:1–3 (Note that in some Bibles these verses are in a different order, following AFTER Chapter 3.)

# FAITH SHARING

In Isaiah 7 the prophet Isaiah encounters Ahaz, the king of Judah. The king is trembling in fear over the news that his city is under attack by his northern neighbors, Israel and Syria. Not only are the city and its inhabitants in danger, but the very existence of the Davidic line is in question. Ahaz has several options: (1) He can join the anti-Assyrian coalition along with Syria and Israel; (2) he can give up his kingship to these attacking kings and hope to survive; (3) he can wage war against them and hope to win; or (4) he can appeal to the Assyrians for help by sending them large amounts of money.

Isaiah's advice is: "Take care you remain tranquil and do not fear; let not your courage fail." Those kings who seem so powerful today will soon lose their power. "Unless your faith is firm, you shall not be firm!" Isaiah tells Ahaz to sit tight, do nothing, wait for the enemies to somehow lose power.

1. What do you think you might have done had you been Ahaz? In your group, share what possible courses of action could be taken—and their consequences. What would a responsible leader do? From whom should a responsible leader seek advice?

2. Then, sit quietly and think about how you yourself react when faced with difficult choices. How do you decide what is the responsible thing to do when faced with several choices that all have uncertain outcomes? Whom do you consult for advice? How would you feel and what would you do if a respected church leader told you to do nothing about a given situation and simply to have faith? After a few minutes, share your personal thoughts within your group. If anything is said during this time that you would like to reflect upon later, note it in your Workbook.

# CLOSING PRAYER

## Hearing the Word

*Leader:*
John and his community had to wrestle with the fact that the majority of Jewish believers did not come to accept Jesus as the Messiah. In our age most people of good will still do not accept him. Yet for some reason he has come into our lives not to judge, not to condemn, but to shine as our light. As we listen to this passage, let us ask ourselves what keeps his light from shining more brightly for us.

## Reading

(All stand, facing the reader.)

*Reader* (picking up the large Bible):
A reading from the gospel according to John (12:37—50).

## Sharing the Light

As the candle is handed to you, stare into the flame and take some time to pray with Jesus silently. When you are finished, pass the candle to the person next to you with the words:

May the light of Christ shine for you!

## Concluding Prayer

*Leader:*
Let us join our hands and pray together as Jesus has taught us.

*All:*
Our Father, . . .
For the kingdom, etc.

*Leader:*
Jesus came into the world as light,
so that everyone who believes in him
might not remain in darkness
now or forever.

*All:*
Amen.


# FOLLOW-UP


## A. Journaling

1. Isaiah's vision of God took place in a setting that was
part of his everyday life, worship in the Jerusalem temple.
He described this vision in terms of what he saw (the Lord
on a throne, like a king), what he heard (the cry of "Holy,
holy, holy!"), what he felt (the shaking of the foundation),
perhaps even what he smelled (the smoke and the incense
in the temple).

Think of a setting that is part of your everyday life in
which you become aware of God's presence. Perhaps it is
a visit to a sister who has just given birth to a baby, at
church during a Lenten observance on Holy Thursday or
Good Friday, at a hospital praying for the survival of a
loved one, a trip to the lake to watch the sunset, or a walk
in your spring garden.

Write about how your senses have helped you to become
more aware of God's presence—holding the baby,

smelling the fresh earth in the garden, seeing the sunset, hearing the peaceful breathing of the person who was ill.

2. God sends Isaiah out to preach to people, telling him that people will not see or hear or understand him. If God asked you to go on such a mission, how would you respond? Write in your journal about how you would talk to God in such a situation.

## B. Additional Resources

1. In *The Catholic Study Bible*, read RG 287–304 for an overview of the main sections and themes of the Book of Isaiah.

2. Read Margaret Nutting Ralph, *Plain Words About Biblical Images*, Chapter III, "The Prophets: Images of God's Word," pp. 84–115. Pages 94–97 talk about the prophets' calls or commissions; pp. 98–101 deal with Isaiah and his children as signs; pp. 108–113 discuss Hosea's children.

3. Read Lawrence Boadt, *Reading the Old Testament*, Chapter 16, "The Great Prophets of the Eighth Century," pp. 309–313, on Assyria's rise to power.

# 4. "God with Us"

### Preparation

- Read Doorly, Chapter 7, "The End of Isaiah's Early Prophetic Activity," and Chapter 8, "The Enthronement of a Prince of Peace."
- Read Isaiah 8–10.
- Reflect on the FOCUS statement and REVIEW OF CONTENTS questions.

---

**FOCUS**

In this session, we will review the chapters which we have read in Isaiah. These chapters in general deal with Isaiah's early career as a prophet. They also begin the transition from Isaiah's early oracles which were addressed to the community at large to that period of Isaiah's ministry when his message was directed more specifically to the Davidic kings. Isaiah acted as an advisor to King Ahaz, and encouraged him to have faith that God would be with him to protect the Davidic line, even when it appeared to be threatened with extinction. We will also reflect on how we become aware of God's presence today.

---

# OPENING PRAYER

## Call to Prayer

*Leader:*
Isaiah proclaimed:
"The people who walked in darkness
have seen a great light." (Is 9:1)

(Leader lights the candle.)

Jesus is the light of the world!

*All:*
The light no darkness can ever extinguish!

## Responsorial Psalm (Is 7:14, 9:5–6; Mt 1:21, adapted)

*Leader:*
As Isaiah and Matthew call us to prayer, let us respond:
For God is with us!

The virgin shall be with child, and bear a son,
and shall name him Immanuel:
for God is with us!

*All:*
For God is with us!

*Leader:*
For a child is born to us,
a son is given us.

*All:*
For God is with us!

*Leader:*
They name him Wonder-Counselor:
his wisdom lives within us.

*All:*
For God is with us!

*Leader:*
They name him God-Hero:
his power lives within us.

*All:*
For God is with us!

*Leader:*
They name him Father-Forever:
his love lives within us.

*All:*
For God is with us!

*Leader:*
They name him Prince of Peace:
his justice lives among us.

*All:*
For God is with us!

*Leader:*
The angel said to Joseph:
You are to name him Jesus,
because he will save his people from their sins.

*All:*
For God is with us!


**Prayer**

*Leader:*
Let us pray quietly and thank God for all the ways in
which Jesus is present to us. (Pause for a whole minute of
reflection.)

*All:*
Blessed are you,
We thank you, Lord our God,
Creator of the universe, Father of Jesus!
In him the age-old longing of your people
has been fulfilled.
A new age has dawned;
the long reign of sin has ended;
a broken world has been renewed.
Anoint us once again with your Spirit,
until we proclaim the good news of Jesus
to all humankind
and the whole earth is filled with his glory.
For he is Lord, now and forever. Amen.

## REVIEW OF CONTENTS

1. Summarize the contents of the first twelve chapters of
the Book of Isaiah as outlined in the following sections:

Chapter 1

Chapters 2–4

Chapter 5:1–7

Chapter 5:11–23

Chapters 6:1–8:18

Chapter 9:2–7

Chapter 9:8–10:4

Chapter 10:5–34

Chapter 11

Chapter 12

2. Answer the following questions about each one of these sections:

a. Why is Chapter 1 called the prologue, and how is it related to the rest of the Book of Isaiah?

b. What is the general content of the early oracles? Give a typical example from this section to illustrate.

c. Identify the following symbolic figures from the song of the vineyard: the owner of the vineyard, the vineyard, the grapes, and the wild grapes.

d. Name one of the reasons for the cries of woe.

e. What events in the life of Isaiah do the memoirs recount?

f. In the passage which deals with the ideal Davidic king, to whom does the phrase "the people who walked in darkness" refer?

g. Why does the author refer to Isaiah 9:8–10:4 as a "liturgy of discipline"?

h. What does it mean to say that Assyria is the "rod" of God's anger?

i. To what does the metaphor "a shoot from the stump of Jesse" refer?

j. Why is Chapter 12 called "a song of praise"?

3. What kind of information can be gained by reflecting on the reference to Uriah the priest in Isaiah 8:1–2, and in 2 Kings 16:10–11?

# VIDEO

Isaiah and the Royal Tradition

As you view the video, please make note of the following:

1. Name one other eighth-century prophet and the focus of his writing.

_____

_____

2. What two elements did Isaiah of Jerusalem particularly emphasize?

_____

_____

3. How has Isaiah's vision of hope been influential?

_____

_____

# BREAK
(10 minutes)

# LEARNING ACTIVITY

1. Have someone in your group read Isaiah 8:1–4 aloud. Answer the following questions based on what was read:

a. What did Isaiah write upon a large tablet?

b. What is the literal meaning of this phrase?

c. This phrase is symbolic of something that will happen. What does it symbolize?

2. Have another person in your group read chapter 8:5–8 aloud. Discuss the following:

a. What symbols does Isaiah use in these verses?

b. What will the waters of the River do? (That is, what will the king of Assyria in all his glory do?)

c. What will happen to the Southern Kingdom, Judah, according to these verses?

3. Compare the fate of Israel, the Northern Kingdom, with the fate of Judah, the Southern Kingdom, as described in 8:1–8.

4. The Hebrew phrase "Immanuel" means "God with us." This phrase appears in Isaiah 7:14 and 8:8. It is also spelled out clearly in Isaiah 8:10. Read the following passages. Discuss what the presence of God means in each passage. Is it a threat or a promise? Is it a blessing or a curse?

– Isaiah 8:9–10

– Isaiah 8:13–14

– Isaiah 9:8–12

– Isaiah 9:18

– Isaiah 10:1–4

– Isaiah 10:12–16

– Isaiah 10:20–21

– Isaiah 10:33

5. After reading the above passages, what conclusions can you draw about what the phrase "God with us" (Immanuel) meant to people in the eighth century?

# FAITH SHARING

In Isaiah's time, the name Immanuel, "God with us," meant different things to different people. To Ahaz, Immanuel was meant to be a sign of hope. "God with us" meant that God would be with Ahaz to protect him, and to protect the Messianic line, from threats of destruction. To Isaiah, "God with us" meant that God would protect Isaiah from "this people," those Judahites who did not support Isaiah's and Ahaz's neutral stand. The Judahites and Israelites who were their enemies would be destroyed by the blazing anger of God's presence. To the proud, arrogant upper class of Israel and Judah, "God with us" meant that God's anger would be with them to lay them low. To the Assyrian king, God's presence brought a wasting sickness to the king's powerful army.

To Jewish Christians of the first century A.D., Immanuel was given yet a different interpretation. Matthew's gospel (Mt 1:23) cites the prophecy of Isaiah 7:14, where the passage in Isaiah is reinterpreted to refer not to a son of Ahaz but to Jesus. To those first Christians, "God with us" meant that Jesus would save people from their sins. In this sense, the sign of Immanuel was a positive promise of hope.

1. With the members of your group, share what you understand by the theme "God with us." Do you see evidence of God's presence in the world today? Is God present to bring hope for the future, or is God present to bring judgment upon sinful people?

2. Are there signs of God's presence in your own life? How do you come to know that these are signs from God? Do you need a prophet or someone else to interpret the meaning of these signs?

3. Perhaps you think that God is not present in the world today as he was in the lives of the ancient Israelites and the first Christians. With the members of your group, share how you think things are different for believers of today and why it may be that God's presence does not seem to be as dynamic a force as it seemed to be for the first Christians.

## CLOSING PRAYER

### Hearing the Word

*Leader:*
John and his community looked forward to a time when the new relationship between humanity and God that began in Jesus would be clearly revealed, when God would clearly be with us, his people. As we listen to this passage, let us ask ourselves who the people are in our lives who reveal to us that God is still with us.

### Reading

(All stand, facing the reader.)

*Reader* (picking up the large Bible):
A reading from the Book of Revelation (22:1–5a).

### Litany of Emmanuel

*All:*
Rejoice! Rejoice! Emmanuel
Shall come to you, O Israel!

## Concluding Prayer

*Leader:*
God of love,
the darkness that covered the earth
has given way to the bright glory of your Word made flesh.
Make us a people of this light.
Make us faithful to your Word,
that we may bring your life to the waiting world.
Grant this through Christ our Lord.

*All:*
Amen.

*Leader:*
The people who walk in darkness
have seen a great light
now and forever and ever.

*All:*
Amen.

# FOLLOW-UP

## A. Journaling

1. The eighth-century prophet Amos describes the presence of God in dramatic fashion. He speaks often of "the day of the Lord," and tells people what this day of the Lord will mean for them. Read Amos 3:13–15, 4:12, 5:14–20, 8:9–12, 9:13–15. In your journal, write about what Amos means when he says, "Prepare to meet your God, O Israel." What does Amos think the presence of God brings to Israel? Imagine that you are a member of the audience hearing these words from Amos. Write about your reaction to Amos's words.

2. Listen to a recording of Handel's *Messiah*. How does Handel interpret Isaiah 7:14 (the contralto recitative), Isaiah 9:1 (the air "The people who have walked in darkness"), Isaiah 9:5 (chorus "For unto us")? After listening to the recording, write about the feelings which these various musical selections evoke. Is the mood somber, joyful, mysterious, ecstatic? How does Handel help you to hear these words from Isaiah anew?

## B. Additional Resources

1. In John W. Miller, *Meet the Prophets*, read Chapters 5, "Amos of Tekoa," and 6, "His Message and Its Relevance," pp. 39–64, for more on the prophet Amos.

2. Read about the theme of Messiah in Margaret Nutting Ralph, *Plain Words About Biblical Images*, Chapter II, "Messiah," pp. 54–83.

# 5. Isaiah Views the Future

## Preparation

- Read Doorly, Chapter 9, "A Shoot from the Stump of Jesse," and Chapter 10, "Oracles Concerning the Nations."
- Read Isaiah 10:5–11:16; 13–23.
- Reflect on the FOCUS statement and REVIEW OF CONTENTS questions.

### FOCUS

In this session, we will examine the political and historical developments within eighth-century Judah. When the Israelites fled the collapsing political situation in the Northern Kingdom with the advance of the Assyrian army, they became known as the "remnant," the survivors of the destruction of that kingdom. Soon the term "remnant" came to take on theological meaning as well; the remnant referred to the northerners who were returning to worship Yahweh with their southern kinfolk in the Jerusalem temple. And by the time of the exile, the remnant referred to all those dispersed peoples who hoped to return to Jerusalem. A similar development can be seen with the term "the branch of Jesse."

We will also see how the long section called "Oracles Concerning the Nations" functioned in the Book of Isaiah. While many people are offended by much of the contents of these oracles, students have much to learn from this body of material about the beliefs and practices of people of the eighth century. We will also learn more about Isaiah's vision of the future, and be able to examine our own beliefs, hopes, and fears about the future of God's people today.

## OPENING PRAYER

### Call to Prayer

*Leader:*
Isaiah proclaimed:
"The Light of Israel will become a fire,
Israel's Holy One a flame,
That burns and consumes." (Is 10:17)

(Leader lights the candle.)

Jesus is the light of the world!

*All:*
The light no darkness can ever extinguish!

### Scripture (Jn 12:12–15)

*Leader:*
Let us listen to John and respond in song as the crowd responded to Jesus: "Blessed is he who comes in the name of the Lord! Hosanna in the highest!"

"When the great crowd that had come to the feast heard that Jesus was coming to Jerusalem, they took palm branches and went out to meet him, and cried out: 'Hosanna!
Blessed is he who comes in the name of the Lord,

[even] the king of Israel.'
Jesus found an ass and sat upon it, as is written:
'Fear no more, O daughter Zion;
see, your king comes, seated upon an ass's colt.'"

*All* (sung refrain):
Blessed is he who comes
in the name of the Lord! Hosanna in the highest!

## Responsorial Psalm (Ps 147:1–6)

*Leader:*
Praise God, who is good;
sing praise to our God, who is gracious.
It is fitting to praise God.
God rebuilds Jerusalem,
gathers the exiles of Israel.

*All* (sung refrain):
Blessed is he who comes
in the name of the Lord! Hosanna in the highest!

*Leader:*
God heals the brokenhearted
and binds up all their wounds.
God knows the number of the stars
and calls them each by name.

*All* (sung refrain):
Blessed is he who comes
in the name of the Lord! Hosanna in the highest!

*Leader:*
Great is our God and mighty in power;
there is no limit to God's wisdom.
Yahweh sustains the lowly
and casts the wicked to the ground.

*All* (sung refrain):
Blessed is he who comes
in the name of the Lord! Hosanna in the highest!


## Prayer

*Leader:*
Let us pray in our hearts that we will be able to welcome
Jesus whenever or however he comes. (Pause for a whole
minute of reflection.)

*All:*
Blessed are you,
We thank you, Lord our God,
Creator of the universe, Father of Jesus!
In him the age-old longing of your people
has been fulfilled.
A new age has dawned;
the long reign of sin has ended;
a broken world has been renewed.
Anoint us once again with your Spirit,
until we proclaim the good news of Jesus
to all humankind
and the whole earth is filled with his glory.
For he is Lord, now and forever. Amen.

# REVIEW OF CONTENTS

1a. There are several different meanings to the term "remnant" in these chapters of Isaiah. Identify the various meanings.

b. Identify the historical, theological, and/or political events with which these various meanings were associated, and show where examples of each meaning can be found in this section of Isaiah.

2a. There are two different ways to translate the Hebrew word *geza*, which occurs in the very first verse of Isaiah 11. What are those two different translations of the word?

1._____

2._____

b. What is the difference between a stump and a stem?

c. How can these differences influence how Isaiah 11:1 is understood, and when the passage is to be dated?

3a. Isaiah 13–23, usually called "Oracles Against the Nations," contains a variety of literary materials. Describe these different types of literature, and give an example of each type from this section of Isaiah.

b. Comment on why the traditional title "Oracles Against the Nations" does not adequately describe the contents of Chapters 13–23.

4. Many people have difficulties with the oracles concerning the nations, both in Isaiah's collection as well as in other prophetic books. What are the stumbling blocks?

5. What value can be derived from reading and studying these oracles?

## VIDEO

The Oracles Concerning the Nations

As you view the video, please make note of the following:

1. Identify at least three characteristics of an oracle against a nation as used in the Bible.

_____

_____

_____

2a. Why was an oracle spoken against Babylon?

_____

_____

b. Against Jerusalem?

_____

_____

## BREAK
(10 minutes)

# LEARNING ACTIVITY

A frequent phrase in the Book of Isaiah which refers to events in the future is "on that day," or the variation, "in days to come." Sometimes it refers to a threatening future (e.g., 2:20, 3:18, 4:1); other times it precedes a promise of hope (e.g., 2:2, 4:2, 10:20). Examine the following passages in Isaiah, and for each passage discuss the questions below in your small group:

Whose future is the passage describing?

Does this passage view the future in a positive or negative light?

Do you think this passage is to be understood as a symbolic or as a literal description of the future? Explain.

– Isaiah 10:5–19

– Isaiah 11:1–9

– Isaiah 11:11

– Isaiah 13:17–22

# FAITH SHARING

Isaiah has many different images of the future. He envisions many promising situations for the future of Israel and Judah, as well as some very threatening and gloomy ones. For those who have harmed God's people, he envisions punishment, vehement curses, violent retribution. The underlying theology is that God is in control of what happens in the world and will reward good behavior, and punish bad.

When you envision your own future, the future of your family (elderly parents, spouse, children), the future of our country, our world, what are your hopes, your fears? Consider how you would complete the following statements to put your answers in perspective.

As you think about your hopes and fears for the future, your wishes for those people whom you cherish, as well as for those who may have caused you harm, keep the poetic images from the Book of Isaiah in mind.

1. Next year, I hope that I will...


2. My wishes for this country are...


3. My hopes for the future of (my children, my spouse, my elderly parents, another) are that...


4. One of my greatest fears for the future is...


5. I have been deeply hurt by (a friend, an employer, a teacher, an intimate friend, a stranger, another). Here is what I wish for this person's future...

# CLOSING PRAYER

## Hearing the Word

*Leader:*
In this passage, Luke and his community portray Peter
preaching on the day of Pentecost. As we listen, let us put
ourselves into the scene as Peter's audience and pray that
we too will respond to his message and his call.

## Reading

(All stand, facing the reader.)

*Reader* (picking up the large Bible):
A reading from the Acts of the Apostles (2:29–41).

## The Laying On of Hands

## Concluding Prayer

*Leader:*
Let us all stand and join hands in prayer.
All-powerful God, Father of our Lord Jesus Christ,
by water and the Holy Spirit
you have freed us from sin
and given us new life.
Send your Holy Spirit upon us once again
to be our helper and guide.

*All sing:*
A multiple Amen!

*Leader:*
Give us the Spirit of wisdom and understanding.

*All sing:*
A multiple Amen!

*Leader:*
Give us the Spirit of right judgment and courage.

*All sing:*
A multiple Amen!

*Leader:*
Give us the Spirit of knowledge and reverence.

*All sing:*
A multiple Amen!

*Leader:*
Fill us with the Spirit of wonder
and of awe in your presence.

*All sing:*
A multiple Amen!

*Leader:*
We ask this through Christ our Lord.

*All sing:*
A multiple Amen! (twice)

*Leader:*
The Light of Israel has become a fire,
Israel's Holy One a flame that burns and consumes
now and forever.

*All:*
Amen.

# FOLLOW-UP

## A. Journaling

1. Many Christmas cards and Christmas celebrations take their theme or motif from the writings of Isaiah. For instance, schoolchildren often make a Jesse tree during Advent to learn about Jesus' ancestors. Many Christmas cards are based on the theme of the lion and the lamb lying down together. (Notice that this reflects an *incorrect* reading of Isaiah 11:6 where it is the *wolf* and the lamb, the *calf* and the lion!) Think about these and other references from the Book of Isaiah that have come to be applied to Jesus, and write about the ones that play an important part of your personal image of Jesus.

2. The oracles against the nations express some violent thoughts about Israel's enemies. Think about situations in which you or someone you loved was harmed, oppressed, persecuted. Write about the feelings you had toward the person or persons who harmed your loved one. Try to imagine what situations could have caused the Israelites to hope for violence against their enemies. Do you find any similarities or differences between your feelings and the strong feelings expressed in Isaiah 13–23?

## B. Additional Resources

1. In *The Catholic Study Bible*, read "Geography of the Holy Land" by Philip J. King, pp. 473–477. Look at the maps, especially Map 5 which pictures the divided kingdoms of Israel and Judah. Identify as many of the places mentioned in the oracle as possible.

2. In *The Catholic Study Bible*, read "Oracles Against the Nations," RG 293.

# 6. Isaiah—The Apocalypse, The Wisdom

## Preparation

- Read Doorly, Chapter 11, "The Apocalypse of Isaiah," and Chapter 12, "A Collection of Oracles."
- Read Isaiah 24–33.
- Reflect on the FOCUS statement and REVIEW OF CONTENTS questions.

---

### FOCUS

In this session, we will study two different sections from the prophecy of Isaiah; the first is the "Apocalypse of Isaiah"— called this because some of the imagery used is similar to the highly symbolic imagery of the apocalyptic literature in Daniel and the Book of Revelation. We will see how Isaiah composed this material to be used in a liturgy which anticipated liberation from Assyria. The second section, a collection of oracles (Chaps. 28–33), comes from the latter part of Isaiah's ministry. These oracles are arranged in an alternating pattern of judgment and hope. Isaiah addressed problems and concerns of the eighth century. He spoke out strongly against any military alliances. He urged Judah's rulers to trust only in God, not in the power of foreign nations. He affirmed the notion that Jerusalem's special status as God's dwelling place meant it could never be destroyed.

---

# OPENING PRAYER

## Call to Prayer

*Leader:*
Isaiah proclaimed:
"Then the moon will blush
and the sun grow pale,
For the LORD of hosts will reign
on Mount Zion and in Jerusalem." (Is 24:23)

(Leader lights the candle.)

Jesus is the light of the world!

*All:*
The light no darkness can ever extinguish!

## Scripture (Rv 1:9–10; 19:6, 9)

*Leader:*
Let us listen to the Apocalypse of John.

I, John, your brother, . . . was caught up in spirit on the Lord's day. . . . Then I heard something like the sound of a great multitude or the sound of rushing water or mighty peals of thunder. . . . Then the angel said to me, "Write this: Blessed are those . . . called to the wedding feast of the Lamb."

*All:*
Blessed are those called
to the wedding feast of the Lamb!

## Responsorial Psalm (Is 25:6–8)

*Leader:*
On this mountain the LORD of hosts
will provide for all peoples
A feast of rich food and choice wines,
juicy, rich food and pure, choice wines.

*All:*
Blessed are those called
to the wedding feast of the Lamb!

*Leader:*
On this mountain he will destroy
the veil that veils all peoples,
The web that is woven over all nations;
he will destroy death forever.

*All:*
Blessed are those called
to the wedding feast of the Lamb!

*Leader:*
The LORD God will wipe away
the tears from all faces;
The reproach of his people he will remove
from the whole earth; for the LORD has spoken.

*All:*
Blessed are those called
to the wedding of the Lamb!

## Prayer

*Leader:*
As Jews and Christians have tried to picture what kind of
future God is preparing for us, we have kept returning to
the image of the wedding feast. Intimacy, faithful love,
shared joy—all are part of this wonderful and endless party.
Let us pray in our hearts for a renewed sense of hope for
the future. (Pause for a whole minute of reflection.)

*All:*
Blessed are you,
We thank you, Lord our God,
Creator of the universe, Father of Jesus!
In him the age-old longing of your people

has been fulfilled.
A new age has dawned;
the long reign of sin has ended;
a broken world has been renewed.
Anoint us once again with your Spirit,
until we proclaim the good news of Jesus
to all humankind
and the whole earth is filled with his glory.
For he is Lord, now and forever. Amen.


## REVIEW OF CONTENTS

1a. Chapters 24–27 of Isaiah are often called the "Apocalypse of Isaiah." Why do many scholars give the section this name?

b. When do scholars date the composition of this section?

2. What are some reasons for not considering these chapters to be apocalyptic?

3. If these chapters are the work of Isaiah of Jerusalem, why would he have composed them? How do they fit into his eighth-century prophesying?

4. Identify some of the ideas and themes of the oracles of Isaiah in Chapters 28–33.

5. What are some of the factors that led people in Judah to believe that Jerusalem would never be destroyed?

## VIDEO

Apocalyptic and Wisdom Genres in Isaiah

As you view the video, please make note of the following:

1. Which characteristic of apocalyptic literature is most striking to you? Why?

_____

_____

2. What characteristic of wisdom literature holds significance for you? Explain.

_____

_____

## BREAK
(10 minutes)

## LEARNING ACTIVITY

1. Have different members in your small group read aloud the following selections from Isaiah 24–27, and then consider these questions:

a. How do you think these selections might have been used in a liturgical celebration?

b. For what events or situations might these readings have been appropriate in Isaiah's time? Explain.

– Isaiah 24:14–16a

– Isaiah 25:1–5

– Isaiah 26:1–4

– Isaiah 27:12–13

2. Identify the features in the following selections that are typical of apocalyptic literature. What kinds of feelings and responses do these selections evoke?

– Isaiah 24:4–8

– Isaiah 24:21–23

– Isaiah 25:6–9

– Isaiah 26:19

– Isaiah 26:20–21

– Isaiah 27:1

3. Read the following sections from Isaiah 28–33. Identify the common theme within each group of oracles. Discuss the message which Isaiah is delivering to his audience by the use of this theme.

a. – Isaiah 28:14–15, 18–19

   – Isaiah 30:1–5

   – Isaiah 31:1–3

b. – Isaiah 28:23–29

   – Isaiah 32:1–8

c. – Isaiah 31:4–5

   – Isaiah 33:20–22

## FAITH SHARING

We have seen that when Isaiah the prophet communicated God's Word to the people of Judah, his religious message was inextricably connected to the politics of the day. We saw that the death of a cruel and powerful emperor was something to celebrate during a worship service. We saw that the capital city of the nation of Judah was under the special protection of God.

1. Do you think that any of the selections in Isaiah 24–27 (a liturgy on the death of Sargon II) would be appropriate for use in your worship services today? Is it appropriate for a Christian community to celebrate an enemy's death? Why or why not?

2. Do you think that God's protection is extended to any particular city or nation today? Does God look after Jerusalem (or any other world capital) today in the same way that God did in the past?

3. Do you think that religious leaders ought to make connections between political issues and religious/faith issues as Isaiah did?

# CLOSING PRAYER

## Hearing the Word

*Leader:*
In the dry Mediterranean region the farmer depends upon irrigation for a crop; the traveler looks forward to the oasis for refreshment. We too know what it is like to be thirsty inside ourselves, to look around for life and hope and see only barrenness. With that kind of thirst let us listen to this passage from the longest apocalyptic section of the New Testament.

## Reading

(All stand, facing the reader.)

*Reader* (picking up the large Bible):
A reading from the Book of Revelation (21:22—22:7).

## Sharing the Water and the Wine

## Concluding Prayer

*Leader:*
Let us gather our prayers together
and give glory to God.

*All:*
Glory be to the Father, etc.

*Leader:*
They will not need light from lamp or sun, for the Lord God shall give them light, and they shall reign forever and ever. (Cf. Rv 22:5.)

*All:*
Amen.

## FOLLOW-UP

### A. Journaling

1. Think about a person or persons who have suffered at the hands of a powerful oppressor. Select one of the poems in Isaiah 24–27. Rewrite this poem so that it could be used as a prayer of thanksgiving by someone today.

2. Read Isaiah 25:6–9. This reading is often used at funeral liturgies. Write about the kinds of feelings that you might have if you heard this reading while mourning the death of a loved one.

### B. Additional Resources

1. In *The Catholic Study Bible*, read "The Revelations," RG 344–347, which deals with apocalyptic literature.

2. Read Revelation 21:1–8, and compare this vision of the new heaven and the new earth with the visions of the future found in Isaiah 25:6–12, 16–19; and 30:19–25.

# 7. The Conclusion of First Isaiah

## Preparation

- Read Doorly, Chapter 13, "Judgment and Salvation," and Chapter 14, "Historical Narratives of Isaiah and Hezekiah."
- Read Isaiah 34–39.
- Reflect on the FOCUS statement and REVIEW OF CONTENTS questions.

---

**FOCUS**

Even though the first part of the Book of Isaiah originated in large part from the prophetic ministry of Isaiah of Jerusalem, there are several sections of Chapters 1–39 which come from later times. The Little Apocalypse (Chaps. 34–35), for instance, is almost certainly from the period of the Babylonian Exile. It is similar in style and content to writings found in Isaiah 40–66. The narrative section in Chapters 36–39 is very different from the idyllic poetry of the previous chapters. While the content of the narrative deals with the time of Isaiah and Hezekiah, the underlying theme and style are more meaningful when read in the light of the time of Josiah and the Deuteronomistic redactors. Once again we are challenged to look at the Book of Isaiah as the result of a complicated process of composition. It is a book which underwent several stages of redaction from the eighth century through the sixth century B.C. to the post-exilic period.

---

# OPENING PRAYER

## Call to Prayer

*Leader:*
Isaiah proclaimed:
"They will see the glory of the LORD,
the splendor of our God." (Is 35:2)

(Leader lights the candle.)

Jesus is the light of the world!

*All:*
The light no darkness can ever extinguish!


## Scripture (Jn 15:4–5)

*Leader:*
Let us listen as John describes the abundance we experience in union with the Lord.

Jesus said:
"Just as a branch cannot bear fruit on its own unless it remains on the vine, so neither can you unless you remain in me. I am the vine, you are the branches. Whoever remains in me and I in him will bear much fruit."

*All:*
Whoever remains in me will bear much fruit!


## Responsorial Psalm (Is 35:1–6a, 10)

*Leader:*
The desert and the parched land will exult;
the steppe will rejoice and bloom.

They will bloom with abundant flowers,
and rejoice with joyful song.

*All:*
Whoever remains in me will bear much fruit!

*Leader:*
The glory of Lebanon will be given to them,
the splendor of Carmel and Sharon;
They will see the glory of the LORD,
the splendor of our God.

*All:*
Whoever remains in me will bear much fruit!

*Leader:*
Strengthen the hands that are feeble,
make firm the knees that are weak,
Say to those whose hearts are frightened:
Be strong, fear not!

*All:*
Whoever remains in me will bear much fruit!

*Leader:*
Here is your God,
he comes with vindication;
With divine recompense
he comes to save you.

*All:*
Whoever remains in me will bear much fruit!

*Leader:*
Then will the eyes of the blind be opened,
the ears of the deaf be cleared;
Then will the lame leap like a stag,
then the tongue of the dumb will sing.

*All:*
Whoever remains in me will bear much fruit!

*Leader:*
Those whom the LORD has ransomed will return
and enter Zion singing,
crowned with everlasting joy;
They will meet with joy and gladness,
sorrow and mourning will flee.

*All:*
Whoever remains in me will bear much fruit!


**Prayer**

*Leader:*
Let us pray quietly that God will bring the new growth in
our lives and in our world to rich fruit. (Pause for a whole
minute of reflection.)

*All:*
Blessed are you,
We thank you, Lord our God,
Creator of the universe, Father of Jesus!
In him the age-old longing of your people
has been fulfilled.
A new age has dawned;
the long reign of sin has ended;
a broken world has been renewed.
Anoint us once again with your Spirit,
until we proclaim the good news of Jesus
to all humankind
and the whole earth is filled with his glory.
For he is Lord, now and forever. Amen.

# REVIEW OF CONTENTS

Identify the following in one or two sentences, telling how each is related to First Isaiah (Chaps. 1–39).

– Little Apocalypse

– Edom

– Lebanon

– Assyria

– Babylon, Babylonia

– Ahaz

– Hezekiah

– Merodach-baladan

– Ashdod rebellion

– Sennacherib

– Rabshakeh

– Josiah

– DH

## VIDEO

Isaiah and the Deuteronomistic Tradition

As you view the video, please make note of the following:

1. How are the accounts in Isaiah 36-39 similar to those in Second Kings? How are they different?

_____

_____


2. In what way does the focus change in the final chapters of First Isaiah?

_____

_____


3. What is the significance of the Lord punishing the proud and rewarding the faithful?

_____

_____


## BREAK
(10 minutes)

# LEARNING ACTIVITY

1. Make two parallel lists in which you write down answers to the following questions after reviewing Isaiah 34 and 35 within your small group.

ISAIAH 34                    ISAIAH 35

a. How is God described? What does God do?

b. With which people is this chapter concerned?

c. What happens to these people?

d. What will happen to the land?

e. How does this chapter end?

2. Compare and contrast these two chapters based on the lists you have compiled. How are the themes of judgment and hope/salvation developed?

# FAITH SHARING

We have seen a pattern of judgment/salvation in many of the chapters of Isaiah 1–39. We have also seen alternating or contrasting messages in which the proud expect success but receive punishment instead. The prayer of Hezekiah in Chapter 38:10–20 has a similar pattern in that it begins with a lament over the fatal illness of Hezekiah, but concludes with a prayer of thanksgiving for recovery.

This type of prayer is called a psalm of thanksgiving. It begins with an expression of deep distress: the person laments his or her state or present condition. Then the mood of the psalm abruptly shifts from bemoaning the evil situation to an expression of thanks to God for alleviating or promising to alleviate the distress.

1. Listen to the first part of this prayer of Hezekiah as your group leader reads it aloud. Have there ever been times in your life when you have been in distress—over a physical ailment or disability, the loss of a spouse or a friend, difficulties with your children, unemployment, or financial problems? Do the sentiments expressed in this part of the prayer match feelings you might have had? Reflect on these questions for a few moments and then share your responses within your small group.

2. Listen to the second part of this prayer, the thanksgiving section, as your group leader reads it aloud. Here the person thanks God for restoration to wholeness, or for the promise of restoration. Think of times in your life when you have been restored, made whole, been transformed. How did you respond? Compare your feelings to the expressions found in this part of the prayer and share them with those in your small group.

3. Have there been times when you prayed for restoration but did not receive an answer to your prayer? Are there

ideas or thoughts in this prayer that you would change, or express differently? Share your reflections with members of your small group.

## CLOSING PRAYER

### Hearing the Word

*Leader:*
In this passage Matthew and his community have John the Baptist's disciples pose the age-old question to Jesus: Are you the one who is to come?

How would we react to the answer Jesus gives them? Where do we fit in his response?

### Reading

(All stand, facing the reader, in anticipation of Jesus' response.)

*Reader* (picking up the large Bible):
A reading from the gospel according to Matthew (11:2–5).

### The Ephphetha

### Concluding Prayer

*Leader:*
We have seen the glory of the Lord,
the splendor of our God,
now and forever.

*All:*
Amen.

# FOLLOW-UP

## A. Journaling

1. People who live in exile have been forced to leave their homes. Sometimes people who have been denied the right to live freely or securely in their own homes also feel like exiles. Have you ever "lived in exile" due to divorce, neighborhood violence, loss of income? Reflect and write on how you would feel if you had been exiled, forced to leave your home.

2. Read through the prayer of Hezekiah (Is 38:10–20). Select one of the lines that was especially meaningful to you during the Faith Sharing activity, and write in your journal about the feelings you had when you heard the lines of the prayer.

3. Isaiah 35 describes the wonderful future for God's people in terms of a flowering desert. This is the kind of imagery which people living on the edge of an arid desert would understand. Rewrite this poem using geographical imagery which would be meaningful to people living in your own time and place.

## B. Additional Resources

1. For background on Josiah and the time of the redacting of Isaiah 36–39, read 2 Kings 22–23:30.

2. In *The Catholic Study Bible*, read "The Deuteronomistic History," RG 116–119.

3. Read Lawrence Boadt, *Reading the Old Testament*, pp. 374–381, for more on the Deuteronomist's History.

# 8. The Unity of the Book of Isaiah

## Preparation

- Read Doorly, Chapter 15, "The Majestic Poet of the Exile (Second Isaiah)," Chapter 16, "Third Isaiah: A Post-Exilic Collection," and Chapter 17, "The Unity of the Book of Isaiah."
- Read Isaiah 40–66.
- Reflect on the FOCUS statement and REVIEW OF CONTENTS questions.

---

### FOCUS

To complete our study of the Book of Isaiah, we will look at some of the main themes of the writings found in Isaiah 40–66. While Chapters 1–39 in general deal with the last half of the eighth century, chapters 40–66 are from a much later period. Chapters 40–55 are attributed to Second Isaiah, an anonymous figure who prophesied to Jews living in exile in Babylon. The message in these chapters is one of joyous anticipation and hopeful expectation. The Persian ruler Cyrus was about to allow the exiles to return home to Jerusalem where they expected to rebuild the city and the temple, and to resume life as they remembered it before the exile. Chapters 56–66, titled Third Isaiah, are from a later time, and are usually considered to be a group of oracles from a variety of different sources. The tone of this section is more somber than that of Second Isaiah. Third Isaiah portrays a community in social, economic, and religious turmoil. While there are many differences among these three sections, there are also several themes which run throughout the Book of Isaiah and give it an overall unity.

---

# OPENING PRAYER

## Call to Prayer

*Leader:*
Isaiah proclaimed:
"Thus says God, the LORD,
I formed you, and set you
as a covenant of the people,
a light for the nations." (Is 42:5–6)

(Leader lights the candle.)

Jesus is the light of the world!

*All:*
The light no darkness can ever extinguish!

*Leader:*
Isaiah has been referred to by Christians as the "fifth evan-
gelist" because of the way that so much of the book could
be read as a foreshadowing of Jesus' career as the Messiah.
As we begin our final session, let us pray together as Christians the last of the Servant Songs of Isaiah.

*Left:*
He was spurned and avoided by men,
a man of suffering, accustomed to infirmity. (Is 53:3)

*Right:*
Judas, one of the Twelve, arrived, accompanied by a large
crowd, with swords and clubs. (Mt 26:47)

*Left:*
Upon him was the chastisement that makes us whole,
by his stripes we were healed. (Is 53:5)

*Right:*
Pilate took Jesus and had him scourged. And the soldiers wove a crown of thorns and placed it on his head.
(Jn 19:1–2)

*Left:*
Oppressed and condemned, he was taken away,
and who would have thought any more of his destiny?
(Is 53:8a)

*Right:*
Carrying the cross himself he went out to what is called the Place of the Skull. . . . There they crucified him.
(Jn 19:17–18)

*Left:*
He was cut off from the land of the living. . . .
A grave was assigned him among the wicked. (Is 53:8b–9)

*Right:*
Taking the body, Joseph wrapped it [in] clean linen and laid it in his new tomb that he had hewn in the rock.
(Mt 27:59)


**Prayer**

*Leader:*
Let us pray quietly for the life and Spirit of Jesus to live within us and give us power. (Pause for a whole minute of reflection.)

*All:*
Blessed are you,
We thank you, Lord our God,
Creator of the universe, Father of Jesus!
In him the age-old longing of your people
has been fulfilled.

A new age has dawned;
the long reign of sin has ended;
a broken world has been renewed.
Anoint us once again with your Spirit,
until we proclaim the good news of Jesus
to all humankind
and the whole earth is filled with his glory.
For he is Lord, now and forever. Amen.


## REVIEW OF CONTENTS

1. Briefly discuss the historical background of the writing of Second Isaiah, and show how Second Isaiah is different from First Isaiah.

2. What is the historical background for the oracles in Isaiah 56–66? Compare and contrast these oracles with those of Isaiah 40–55.

3. Identify the main themes of Second Isaiah.

4. Identify the main themes of Third Isaiah, and show how these are similar to or different from those of Second Isaiah.

5. What are the unifying themes which run throughout the Book of Isaiah?

# VIDEO

The Influence of Isaiah

As you view the video, please make note of the following:

1. What application of the Isaian tradition found in the New Testament is most meaningful to you? Explain.

_____

_____

2. How did Isaiah influence the bishops' peace pastoral and the Vatican document, *Gaudium et Spes*?

_____

_____

# BREAK
(10 minutes)

# LEARNING ACTIVITY

1a. Have a member of your small group read Isaiah 30:12–14 aloud. Imagine that you are listening to Isaiah preach this message. What is God saying through his prophet Isaiah to this audience? What effect might these words have had on the audience?

b. Now, have someone else in your group read Isaiah 40:1–2 aloud. Imagine that you are part of an audience hearing this message. What is God saying here? What effect would such words have on the audience?

2. Look up the following passages from First (Chaps. 1–39) and Second (Chaps. 40–55) Isaiah, and answer these questions:

a. Which military and world leaders are mentioned?

b. What does the passage reveal about these world powers?

– 8:7–8

– 10:5–6, 16

– 20:1–6

– 31:1–3

– 36:1, 13–16; 37:33–35

– 41:25

– 43:14–15

– 44:28

– 45:1–4

– 47:5–6

c. According to the theology of First and Second Isaiah, God has complete power over all the world powers and military leaders just cited in the preceding passages. Yet, God does not treat them all in the same way. What accounts for the difference?

3. Read the following passages from Third Isaiah (Chaps. 56–66) and discuss what each reveals about everyday life in Jerusalem after the return from exile.

– 56:2–7

– 57:13

– 58:4–7

– 58:12; 61:4; 63:18; 64:10–11

– 59:3–4, 12–14

– 65:3–5

# FAITH SHARING

1. Before I studied the book of Isaiah I never knew that...

2. Something that really challenges me as a result of our study is...

3. After reading Isaiah, I was very comforted to learn...

4. Our problems today are very similar to (or very different from) conditions during the time of Isaiah because...

5. One thing I learned about myself from my reading of Isaiah is...

6. A passage from Isaiah that now means a lot to me as a result of our study is...

# CLOSING PRAYER

## Hearing the Word

*Leader:*
As we listen to this passage from Luke, let us put ourselves in the place of the people in the synagogue that Sabbath day and try to hear Jesus' message with a new freshness and power. What are the "gracious words" that he is speaking to you right now?

## Reading

(All stand, facing the reader.)

*Reader* (picking up the large Bible):
A reading from the gospel according to Luke (4:14–22).

## The Anointing

*Leader:*
As we come to the end of these sessions together, let us pray that the Spirit's power will live in us and work through us as we go forth. As we anoint each other with this oil, we will say to each other:

The Spirit of God has anointed you and sent you!

To this reminder together we will add in song our Amen!

## Concluding Prayer

*Leader:*
The Spirit makes us one Body in Christ. Let us join hands and pray together as Jesus has taught us.

*All:*
Our Father,...
For the kingdom, etc.

*Leader:*
The Lord God says to us:
I have formed you, and set you
as a covenant of the people,
a light for the nations,
now and forever.

*All:*
Amen.

# FOLLOW-UP

## A. Journaling

1. Select one of the passages that has been especially meaningful to you as a result of your study of Isaiah. Read this passage over carefully. Write in your journal about your thoughts and feelings and why this passage has caught your attention.

2. Think about the responses of different members of your study group to the Book of Isaiah. What were some insights you learned about the Book of Isaiah from the group members' sharing? Write down some of these ideas and your thoughts about the experience of sharing God's Word in a community of believers.

3. Think about questions which may have arisen as the result of your study. What would you like to know about the Book of Isaiah, or about prophecy, or about the composition of a book of the Bible? Make a list of those things which you would like to continue to investigate. Pick one of these things. Write about what you could do to learn more about it.

## B. Additional Resources

1. In Lawrence Boadt, *Reading the Old Testament*, read Chapter 20, "Sing Us a Song of Zion!," pp. 405–430, for more about Second Isaiah.

2. Also in Lawrence Boadt, *Reading the Old Testament*, read Chapter 21, "The Struggle to Restore the Land (540–500 B.C.)," pp. 431–447, for more about the post-exilic period and Third Isaiah.